Cuauhtémoc Blanco

To the Top!

2012 Joins the Dorados de Sinaloa team.

2011 Champion of the Second Division Clausura Tournament with Irapuato.

2010 Goes to the Irapuato from the Second Division.

2009 Joins the Veracruz of Mexico.

2008 MVP of the MLS' Stars Game.

2007 Wins the Golden Ball; joins the Chicago Fire.

2006 Champion of the CONCACAF's Champions Cup with Club América.

2005 Champion of the Clausura Tournament with Club América; wins the Golden Ball.

2004 Scores his hundredth goal in Mexican soccer.

2001 Sits out for eight months.

2000 Joins the Valladolid of Spain.

1999 Champion of the Confederations Cup, scoring in the final game.

1998 Most goals in the Mexican league and champion of the Golden Cup.

1997 Joins Necaxa, after leaving the América.

1996 Champion of the Golden Cup.

1995 Makes his debut with the Mexican national team.

1992 Makes his debut in the Mexican First Division with Club América.

1990 Cuauhtémoc makes it to the juvenile division of Club América.

1973 Cuauhtémoc Blanco Bravo is born in Tlatilco, Mexico D.F. on January 17.

Mason Crest
370 Reed Road
Broomall, Pennsylvania 19008
www.masoncrest.com

Printed and bound in the United States of America.

First printing
9 8 7 6 5 4 3 2 1

Series ISBN: 978-1-4222-2647-6
ISBN: 978-1-4222-2667-4
ebook ISBN: 978-1-4222-9208-2

Library of Congress Cataloging-in-Publication Data

Elzaurdia, Paco.
  Cuauhtémoc Blanco / by Paco Elzaurdia.
      p. cm.
  ISBN 978-1-4222-2667-4 (hardcover) – ISBN 978-1-4222-2647-6 (series hardcover) – ISBN 978-1-4222-9208-2 (ebook)
  1. Blanco, Cuauhtémoc, 1973–Juvenile literature. 2. Soccer players–Mexico–Biography–Juvenile literature. I. Title.
  GV942.7.B54E59 2013
  796.334092–dc23
  [B]
                                  2012031766

ABOUT THE AUTHOR:
PACO ELZAURDIA was born in Montevideo, Uruguay and is an independent writer and editor. He has been the General Editor for *La Vision* (*the Vision*), a newspaper in Georgia, United States, and works as freelance for magazines and newspapers. He is also correspondent for the Argentinian sports magazine *Olé* and director of the Atlanta's soccer newspaper *Contra Ataque*.

PICTURE CREDITS:
EFE Photos: 1, 4, 6, 8, 10, 11, 12, 13, 14, 16, 17, 18, 21, 22, 23, 24, 26, 27
Hefebreo | vivodefutbol.com: 28

SUPERSTARS OF SOCCER

Cuauhtémoc Blanco

CONTENTS

CHAPTER 1: Mexican Idol   5
CHAPTER 2: Cuau's Teams   9
CHAPTER 3: National and Beyond   19
CHAPTER 4: A Star On and Off the Field   25
FIND OUT MORE   30
GLOSSARY   31
INDEX   32

Mexican Idol

Cuauhtémoc Blanco Bravo is a one of a kind star. He's famous for a lot of reasons. Blanco is an amazing soccer player. He's played very well for the Mexican national team. He handles himself well in front of the press and coaches. Blanco even stars in **SOAP OPERAS**!

Blanco, or "Cuau," as he is sometimes called, is one of the biggest soccer stars in Mexico. Mexicans and soccer fans everywhere watch him to see what his next move will be. It doesn't matter what Mexican league team fans root for. They can look past team colors to cheer for Blanco.

One soccer expert put it this way: "Do you know why Cuauhtémoc is such a good player? He does not care whether he is playing against Puebla or Germany. He only cares about playing." Blanco shows his love for playing soccer every time he steps onto the field.

A STAR IS BORN

Cuauhtémoc Blanco was born on January 17, 1973. His name means, "One that descends like an eagle" in Nahuatl, an **INDIGENOUS LANGUAGE**. He was born in Tlatilco, a part of Mexico City (the capital of Mexico). Cuauhtémoc and his family lived in Tlatilco for a few years. But soon, the family moved to Tepito, the place Cuauhtémoc truly calls home.

The young Blanco started playing soccer while living in Tepito. He joined a team called the Impala. He and the team played in a big **TOURNAMENT** that would change Blanco's life. At the tournament, a talent scout saw him play. The scout knew that he was watching a young soccer star and decided to have him play in a new club.

The scout worked for Club América (also called the Eagles). Blanco had wanted to play for the team for his whole life. His favorite players played for Club América. And now he'd be trying out for the team, too.

Blanco made the team, but at first he didn't get the position he wanted. At the next round of tryouts, how-

Just about every Mexican soccer fan knows who Cuauhtémoc Blanco is.

ever, Blanco got to play the position he wanted. He started playing **MIDFIELD** in Club América's youth league. He even signed a three-year deal with the team.

THE BIG FIELD

December 2, 1992 was a big day for Blanco. He began playing on Club América's First Division team. He had worked his way up from the youth division and earned a spot on the team.

Club América was playing the Lions, another Mexican team. During the second half of the game, the Eagles coach decided that it was time to put Blanco in. The game ended up tied, but there was no going back for Blanco. He had his first taste of playing for América's First Division team.

Three months later, Blanco scored his first goal with the First Division. The star midfielder was just getting started, though. Over the next two years, Cuauhtémoc started to make it onto the field more often.

A new coach began working with Club América. He realized how good a player Blanco was and made him into a starter. Now Blanco got to play even more. He played the whole season, and was even named "Rookie of the Season" in 1994–1995. América tripled his pay. The team also signed him onto a longer contract to keep him for a few more years.

The Mexican League

Mexican soccer teams are split up into divisions. The First Division is made up of the top teams and players. Each year, there are two championships, the Apertura (Opening) in the winter, and the Clausura (Closing) in the summer.

Blanco is used to celebrating wins with his teammates after years of playing.

CHAPTER 2

Cuau's Teams

Although América had given him his start in soccer, Cuau didn't stay with the team long. Soon, he started to think about moving to other teams. He might not have known it then, but Blanco would move to many different teams during his career.

SHINING

In 1997, Blanco left the Eagles and moved to the Rayos of Necaxa. He kept on improving with his new team. Some even argued that he was the best player in the country. To prove it, Blanco won the Citlali award for best player in the 1998 Winter Tournament.

One year later, Blanco came back to Club América. After leaving the team, Blanco had learned a lot and had become a better player. But it was time for him to go back to the team he had played with for so many years. This time, Blanco stayed with Club América until 2000. Playing for América, he reached even greater heights. Blanco scored sixteen goals during the 1998 season. He was the highest-scoring player of any team.

In 2000, Blanco and América shined during the Copa Libertadores (Champions of America Cup). Blanco scored nine goals himself during the tournament, giving the team an edge. In the first game, Club América defeated the Olympia from Paraguay by 8–2. América lost to the Boca Juniors, but managed to stay in the tournament.

The final game almost went down to the last second. Unfortunately for América, the other team scored a goal and the Eagles lost. Even though his team didn't win, Blanco played very well throughout the Copa. He scored the most goals in the Copa Libertadores of any Mexican player in history. There was no stopping Cuau!

A NEW CHALLENGE

Blanco was just starting his career in soccer, but he'd already achieved a lot in just a few years. He had a lot of great things left to do, too!

In 2000, fans began talking about Blanco leaving Club América. Many people believed he was going to play in Spain.

Blanco would make less money in Europe. And a lot of people thought that Mexican soccer players weren't good enough to get signed by European teams. But Blanco liked the challenge. He wanted to show everyone that he had the skills to play in Europe. He signed a contract with Real Vallodolid in Spain.

Blanco didn't have to wait long to show fans that his move to Real Vallodolid was the right choice. In September of 2001, he scored a huge goal. Valladolid was playing the powerful Real Madrid. With just two minutes left in the game, Cuau surprised the other team with a kick that scored a tying goal.

Meanwhile, back in Mexico, Club América won the 2002 Summer Tournament. Blanco had never won the tournament. He'd never won a Mexican **CHAMPIONSHIP**. And now Blanco's old team had done it, right after he left.

RETURN

Blanco only stayed in Spain for two seasons. He missed his home country. He also wasn't doing as well as everyone had expected. Although Blanco had a few great moments, he wasn't playing as well as he knew he could.

Blanco decided to go back to Club América. That same year, América

Cuau was ready for the challenge of playing with Valladolid in Spain.

Coaches and teammates have all had an influence on Blanco, and have helped make him into the star he is today.

Mexican soccer fans take their sport seriously.

made it to the semifinals in the Copa Libertadores. It wasn't going to be Cuau's lucky year, though. His team lost to Sao Caetano of Brazil and was knocked out of the tournament.

Two years later, América was playing the same team in the Copa Libertadores semifinals. This time, the game took an ugly turn. The game ended in a 1–1 tie. One thing led to another, and the players got into a fight. Even coaches and fans joined in!

People blamed Blanco for starting the fight. He had been kicked out of the game earlier for hitting another player with his elbow. Club América was banned from the stadium for a few games. The team was also kept from playing in South American Soccer Confederation (CONMEBOL) tournaments for one year.

MORE BACK AND FORTH

In 2004, Blanco left Club América again. But the very next year, he came back. He just couldn't stay away from the team that had given him his first shot at **PROFESSIONAL** soccer.

When Blanco came back to Club América, the team had many star players. América had a real shot at winning the League championship in 2005. Blanco hadn't won a championship before, but many fans thought 2005

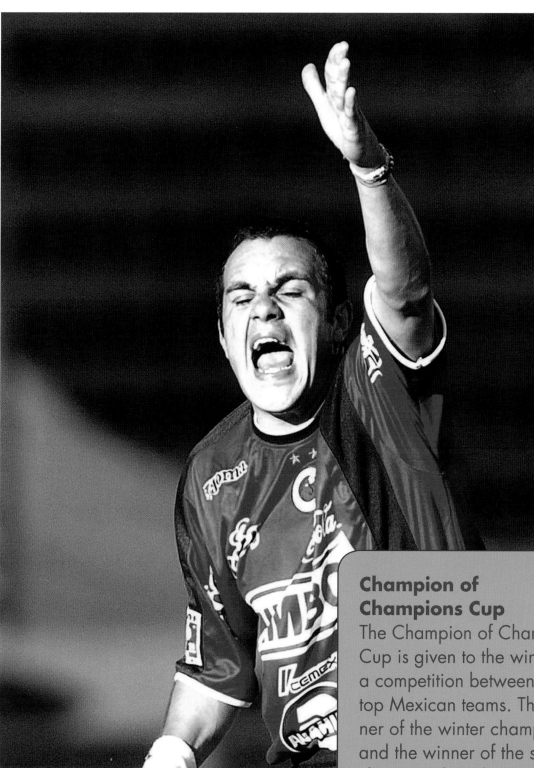

Blanco gives it his all on the field.

Champion of Champions Cup
The Champion of Champions Cup is given to the winner of a competition between the two top Mexican teams. The winner of the winter championship and the winner of the summer championship play each other. Whoever wins gets the Champion of Champions cup. Blanco and Club América won the Cup in 2005.

Blanco does what it takes to win.

might be his year. In front of more than 100,000 fans, América won the final game of the tournament, 6–3.

Blanco didn't have the best season in 2006. The Mexican national team didn't do well in that year's World Cup. Mexico lost to Barcelona, and then Egypt knocked the team out of the Cup. Blanco still hadn't won a World Cup.

WELCOME TO THE USA

Blanco never seemed to play with one team for long. He had left and returned to Club América twice. Now, he was leaving the team for a third time.

In 2007, Blanco began a new international journey. In April, he moved to the United States to play in Major League Soccer (MLS). He was going to play for a team called the Chicago Fire. The Fire was excited to have the Mexican star join the team. Blanco was popular with soccer fans in the United States, especially with Mexican and Mexican American fans. Many of them came to Chicago's soccer stadium to watch him play.

Blanco started off the season strong. He scored two goals in his very first two games. He was almost a one-man show in Chicago. During his first season with the Fire, he was almost named **MOST VALUABLE PLAYER (MVP)**.

By 2008, Blanco was definitely a star. He signed the second-biggest contract in the MLS. Only David Beckham, the famous British player, earned more money. Blanco was making more than $2.5 million!

Blanco was also voted the MVP of the 2008 **ALL-STARS GAME**. One side was made up of the best players in the MLS. The other team was West Ham United, from England. Blanco scored a goal and an assist. He helped his team win, 3–2.

The soccer season in the United States is short. Cuau still had time to play some soccer in the Mexican play-offs after the end of the U.S. season.

HOME

Blanco returned to Mexico for good in 2009. He decided not to stay with the Chicago Fire. Mexico was his home, after all.

Blanco had a surprise in store for fans, though. He joined a Second Division team, rather than one in the First Division. His new team was Veracruz, the Sharks. Some people had thought he would go back to Club América again.

Just like in the past, Blanco kept moving around. In 2009 and 2010, he played for the Sharks. In 2011, he moved on to Irapuato, another team in the Second Division. He helped the team win the Second Division championship.

Blanco's time with Irapuato didn't end well. The Club didn't pay him! Blanco wasn't happy. He didn't like letting his fans down, even when it wasn't his fault.

Today, Blanco plays for the Dorados de Sinaloa. Dorados are also a Second Division team. No one knows for sure whether Blanco will **RETIRE** with the

Playing for Different Countries

Soccer players can actually play for different countries. Andrés Guardado has played for both Mexican and Spanish league teams. Teams are free to sign players from any country. Only certain people qualify to play on national teams, though. Players have to be citizens of the country they play for. Guardado, for example, only qualifies to play on Mexico's national team in international competitions like the World Cup.

Even when he's playing in other countries, Blanco always come back to Mexico to play for the national team.

CHAPTER 3

National and Beyond

Cuauhtémoc Blanco made a name for himself playing soccer in Mexico. But he's also a big star outside of Mexico. He's good enough to play for Mexico's national team. The team is also known as the "Tri." The team got its name from the three colors on the uniforms Mexican players wear—red, white, and green.

Cuau is one of the most famous Tri members. He started playing on the national team in February of 1995, at the start of his career. Blanco was a big part of the team for many years.

TIME FOR THE CUPS

When Blanco was playing at his best, Mexico's national team also succeeded. Blanco had some of his best years between 1995 and 2000. During that time, he helped make the Tri a truly great team.

In 1996, Mexico defeated Brazil in the Confederation of North, Central American, and Caribbean Association Football (CONCACAF) Gold Cup grand final. Blanco scored one of two goals for the win. Then, two years later, Mexico won the Gold Cup again, beating the United States.

Blanco also played in several America Cups around the same time. His first was in 1997, in Bolivia. In the first game of the Cup, Mexico faced Colombia. The Tri beat Colombia by two goals, and went on to the next round. The team lost that game, 3–2, but tied the next one. Mexico ended up qualifying for second place.

In the quarterfinal, Cuau scored a goal that tied the game. It was his first goal in the America Cup. Mexico won in the quarterfinals and went on to the semifinals. The Tri lost the next game, but then beat Peru for third place.

Two years later, Mexico was back to the America Cup in Paraguay. The team won a few games and lost a few. The Tri's performance earned the team third place again.

Blanco didn't make it back to the America Cup until 2007. Mexico won third place again that year!

STAR OF THE TEAM

Blanco had become a soccer star and one of the best players on the Tri. He is the all-time highest scorer during the Confederations Cup. He has scored nine goals in his time at the Cup. Blanco has also scored five goals in the America Cup, too. Only Luís Hernández has scored more goals in the Cup.

In all, Blanco has scored thirty-nine goals in official matches with Mexico's national team. He has the second highest number of goals in the history of the Tri.

Soccer fans everywhere know that Blanco is a great player. A lot of them were upset, though, when Blanco didn't make it onto the Mexican World Cup team in 2006. Fans were angry about the decision. They thought he should have gone.

Though he didn't make the team in 2006, Blanco got to play in more competitions. In 2007, he played in both the Gold Cup and the America Cup. One year later, he made it onto the 2010 World Cup team.

Blanco has played for the national team 119 times. Only five other players in the team's history have played in more games.

WORLD CUPS

Blanco has played in three World Cups since he started playing soccer. He has played in eleven World Cup games and scored three goals during the Cup.

Blanco is one of only three Mexican players who have scored in two back-to-back World Cups. Even better, Blanco is the only Mexican player to have scored a goal in every World Cup he's played in.

His very first World Cup was in France, in 1998. Mexico faced some very talented teams. The Tri beat South Korea 3–1. Blanco helped tie the next game, even though the Tri were behind by two points. It was his first goal in a World Cup. The next game was more of the same. Mexico tied the game, coming from behind.

Although Mexico had pulled out some amazing moves, the team didn't get much farther. The Tri lost to Germany, and were sent home. But Blanco was proud—he had played in his first World Cup, and had even scored a goal.

Blanco had another chance in 2002. This time, the World Cup was held in Japan. Blanco scored in the very first game against Croatia, helping win the game. The Tri won the next game, too, and even tied with Italy in the third game. But then Mexico fell to their rivals, the United States. Once again, Mexico was sent home.

Blanco wasn't sure if he would get to go to a third World Cup. He told Goal. com, "I'm not assured of a World Cup spot. I have to earn it with the way I play with my team. If I'm able to play there, I know it will be my last World

Blanco called the Chicago Fire home for a little while, playing soccer in the United States.

Blanco is an experienced Tri player.

Blanco knows he has to earn a spot on the national team.

Cup and I have to prepare in order to arrive well. I'm going to contribute to the team the way I've always done it, with all the teams I've played on, on all the national team rosters I've been part of."

Blanco ended up making the team. He was headed to his third World Cup in South Africa. This time, Blanco was thirty-seven. That's getting old for soccer players! Some fans weren't sure whether he was in good enough shape to play in such a big competition. Cuau knew he was up to the challenge, though.

Mexico played South Africa in the very first game of the World Cup. Play-

ers from both felt the pressure of playing first! In the end, the two teams tied. In the second game, Mexico easily beat France. Blanco scored his third World Cup goal during the game. Soon, the Tri had to face Argentina. In 2006, Argentina had knocked Mexico out of the World Cup. What would happen this time?

Mexico was winning for a little while. But then Argentina came back with two goals. Mexico's World Cup journey was over.

Blanco owes his success to his own talent and hard work, along with the work of his coaches, teammates, and friends.

CHAPTER 4

A Star On and Off the Field

There are lots of headlines about Cuauhtémoc Blanco in the news. He's a great soccer player, but he also makes news off the field. Blanco isn't afraid to say whatever he wants to reporters. He's starred in a soap opera. He argues with other players or coaches. Soccer fans seem to be just as interested in what Cuau does on and off the field.

Fans never know what Blanco's going to do next. He can be as surprising as the game of soccer itself. For example, the Feyenoord team of Rotterdam was interested in signing Blanco after the 1998 World Cup. Instead, Blanco just disappeared on vacation. No one could find him!

LIGHTS, CAMERA, ACTION

Soccer fans aren't the only people interested in Blanco. People will watch him whether he's on the field or on a soap opera. In 2010 and 2011, Blanco played "Juanjo" in a Mexican soap opera. He made $20,000 each month for his work.

Blanco's character Juanjo ended up dying in the show. But fans loved Cuau and his character so much, that the show had to bring him back. Juanjo is

Blanco's most famous role. Before that, he acted in another soap opera in 2009. He won awards for his performance on the show *Until the Money Do Us Part*.

For a little while, Cuau had his own show, called *The Cuauhtémoc Blanco Hour*. Celebrities and sports stars were invited to the show.

Blanco isn't a stranger to radio either. He had his own radio program called *Direct to Blanco*. During the show, he just talked about whatever was on his mind that day. Fans loved it.

The Gold Cup

The Gold Cup is a contest between soccer teams from North America, Central America, the Caribbean, and some South American countries. It is held every two years. Every other Gold Cup also leads to the World Cup. The top three teams in the Gold Cup get to go to the World Cup. Mexico and the United States have won the most Gold Cups in recent years.

Two soccer legends come together—coach Hugo Sánchez and Cuauhtémoc Blanco.

CONTROVERSIAL

Blanco is always good for a show off the field. Fans from around the world hear about his **CONTROVERSIAL** actions and words.

In November of 1998, Blanco's wife Mariela Santoyo said Cuau tried to hurt her. They had gotten into a fight that went too far. Later, Blanco and his wife claimed it was a misunderstanding.

Fans find Cuau's antics off the field just as entertaining as his playing.

Blanco still has a few more wins to celebrate before he retires.

Trademark Trick

Blanco is famous for his move called the "cuauhtemina" or "Cuau trick." He first tried it in the 1996 World Cup. As two players from the South Korean team closed in on him, Blanco passed between them with the ball caught between his feet. Fans have come to know and love this trademark move, which he uses on the field from time to time.

Blanco is known for partying, too. He has gotten in trouble a few times for getting caught having a party before big games, when he and his teammates should be thinking about the game.

Through all the controversies, Cuau isn't afraid to say exactly what he's thinking. He frequently tells people he doesn't like them, on camera. He says what he thinks about coaches and other players. He has even called a couple of people "rats." Blanco says what is on his mind, no matter who is listening.

Wherever he goes, Cuau is in the spotlight. From Mexico, to Spain, to the United States, Blanco is famous around the world.

Like any player, Blanco's had some games that he'd like to forget. But the soccer star has also had more than his fair share of great games. He's used moves that fans will remember for a long time. Blanco is one of the most interesting Mexican players in a long time. He is also one of the most controversial.

Though Blanco is close to the end of his career, fans are still watching him. He still has games left to play, and you can be sure that fans will be hanging on his every move! He's truly a part of Mexican soccer history.

FIND OUT MORE
On the Internet

ESPN.COM SOCCER NEWS

espn.go.com/sports/soccer

FIFA.COM MEXICO

www.fifa.com/associations/association=mex/index.html

FIFA PLAYER STATISTICS

www.fifa.com/worldfootball/statisticsandrecords/players/player=162580

GOAL.COM MEXICAN SOCCER NEWS

www.goal.com/en-us/news/114/mexico

SQUIDOO

www.squidoo.com/CuauhtemocBlanco

GLOSSARY

ALL-STARS GAME: A Major League Soccer game held once a year in which the league's best players play together against another team.

ASSIST: A pass that leads to a goal.

CHAMPIONSHIP: A competition between two soccer teams.

CONTROVERSIAL: If something is controversial, people have many different opinions about it.

INDIGENOUS LANGUAGE: A language (spoken word) that comes from a specific area and is spoken by people that originally come from that area.

MIDFIELD: The center of the soccer field. Midfielders play in between forwards and defensive players.

MOST VALUABLE PLAYER (MVP): The award given to the best player in a sports competition, usually a tournament or league finals.

PROFESSIONAL: Professionals are paid for their work.

RETIRE: To end a career.

SOAP OPERAS: Dramas performed on radio or television, often with twisting stories and many characters.

TOURNAMENT: A series of games played to choose a winner.

INDEX

All-Stars Game 15

Club América 5, 7, 9–10, 12–13,
    15, 17
Copa Libertadores (Champions of
    America Cup) 9, 12
cuauhtemina 29

Direct to Blanco 25

First Division 7, 15, 17

Gold Cup 19–20, 26

Major League Soccer (MLS) 15, 31

Mexico City 5
Most Valuable Player (MVP) 15

Nahuatl 5

Rayos of Necaxa 9

Santoyo, Mariela 27
South American Soccer
    Confederation (CONMEBOL) 12

Until the Money Do Us Part 25

World Cup 15–16, 20, 23, 25–
    26, 29